Corrupt Business Practices in Newspaper Circulation

The Eye-opening Experiences of a Newsboy

By: James M. Lowrance © 2010

2

Dedicated to all of the honest, hard working newspaper carriers throughout the world.

TABLE OF CONTENTS:

INTRODUCTION:

(Note: Neither the name of the publishing company I make reference to nor any of its employees or representatives will be named in this book.)

During the decades starting in the 1980s and into the first decade of the 2000s, I worked for four different newspaper and magazine publications, including being hired as a district manager for one of them – a position I held for only a couple of weeks (more on this story later). Even people, who know me personally, will not be able to determine with certainty, which newspaper publication I will be referring-to, regarding corrupt business practices that I will describe as being perpetrated by them.

In my opinion, it doesn't matter at this point, who the company was. What ultimately matters, is that people working for companies either as employees or under contracts with them, should be willing to stand up for their rights under the laws of the United States and that legislation continues to allow the opportunity for Americans to reasonably register complaints for investigation when necessary.

In-short, dishonest business practices should be exposed for what they are.

Legitimate Complaints

Certainly a reasonable degree of screening must also occur, so that bogus complaints by irate, disgruntled or vindictive employees are not given undue credence. Those with legitimate complaints however, that are well-documented should not feel intimidated against registering these when necessary. They should also not be made to feel that simply wanting to see accountability for corrupt business practices by a company, with no further personal gain sought by them, is going to come at a personal financial cost to them. They should also not feel they are in danger of reprisals by a company or by those directly or indirectly associated with them for registering a legitimate complaint. It should also be recognized that employees can be the source of corruption in a company as well and can be guilty of cheating their employers. Opportunity for companies to seek accountability in these cases is equally important.

Seeking Remedies

I did take a degree of action by registering complaints against the company I refer-to in this book, through a mediating bureau. This was the only amount of time I was willing to invest in attempt to see possible accountability result and changes that might result from it. My reason for reluctance in taking further action was based on the fact that I have seen far too-much unwillingness on the part of others affected by unethical business behaviors to seek remedies for them. Collaboration is often essential in cases such as mine that I will describe in the chapters that follow but the cooperation by those of like-complaints was simply not available to me.

This brought me to the realization that most people affected by corrupt business practices would rather simply walk away from them afterward, as opposed to "getting involved" in trying to change them or to bring accountability to companies for perpetrating them. This, despite the fact that we don't attempt to influence changes only for the sake of ourselves but also for the sake of others who might also be affected.

My Inspiration for this Book

In some ways I regret not having done more in my case, after so many years of witnessing this type of thing which is largely the inspiration behind this book. I also feel that the type practices I will describe that included illegitimate methods for increasing circulation by some newspaper companies, is far more common than the general public may realize. This also means that the cost of advertising being purchased from these newspapers, by businesses and consumers is sometimes illegitimately inflated by dishonest companies, based on false circulation numbers. Could it be that this is possibly one of the reasons for the continuing downfall of printed newspapers, with honest ones suffering, along with the dishonest ones?

It often takes collaborating experiences to get the attention of those who investigate and prosecute or penalize illegal business activities, such as those I have just described. In many cases, those who try to get the ball rolling on an investigation of a company, will find their selves alone and are afterward pegged as "whistle blowers".

This is unfortunate and the very reason these type business practices continue in companies and often progressively increase when accountability is lacking. I believe this "ripple effect" – if you will, affects all types of businesses to some degree and also those who are in public office positions, from small town governments to the higher offices of government service.

Recognizing Honest Businessmen

At the same time, there are many honest and highly ethical people in these businesses, and offices, including those in the newspaper industry but honesty can only maintain an upper-hand when accountability for potential dishonestly remains in place and is practiced when necessary. It is my belief as a Christian and believer in a God who judges the actions of all men and women that accountability does eventually occur as a result of what we might call "the reaping process" even when accountability within a company is lacking. It is my personal belief that not one person escapes the reward or the punishment for both the good and evil practices they commit during their lifetimes.

Some believers in the inescapable and inevitable process of judgment and reward simply refer to it using the term "justice prevails" and I am certainly a believer of this statement.

In the chapters of this book that follow, I will relate my experiences as a contract carrier for a newspaper, during which time I witnessed an alarming frequency of corrupt business practices that in many cases directly affected me and my family as well as fellow contract workers and employees of the company.

CHAPTER ONE

Why I became a Newsboy

Being a newspaper distributor is something I would have never guessed earlier in my life, to be an occupation I would eventually hold for over 16 years however, life-circumstances, including some very positive ones, brought me to the eventual destiny of becoming a "newsboy".

My duties on the job included distribution of newspapers to stores and newspaper racks, in addition to home subscribers. The only difficult aspect of the job, was the detailed paperwork involved in keeping singly copy circulation (outlet sales) and home delivery subscriber circulation recorded as well as a record of unsold newspapers (returns) for which I was given credit. Surprisingly, the income for this occupation was quite good, which gave me ample daytime hours to successfully pursue the marketing of a fishing tackle accessory, product-invention and to further my writing profession. Despite this fact, there were many times I found myself having to battle corrupt business practices.

In some cases this negatively affected my own income by 1,000s of dollars and that often required my relentless persistence to see correction of them and past-due credit balances paid back to me.

My Former Occupations

In the year 1989, I formed a small corporation in my hometown to market a fishing tackle accessory that I invented in partnership with my brother-in-law. I involved local businessmen who agreed to finance the product-invention, so that it would be under a patent pending status, placed in packaging for retail sales and properly covered by product liability insurance, required by major retail chain stores and outlets. I was a specialty foods salesman at the time, working many hours and traveling 100s of miles per week, which made it difficult to invest the time that was needed to successfully market the product invention.

My wife was also pregnant at the time, with our second child – a daughter, who would be born in 1990. The pregnancy was a difficult one however, with my wife suffering premature dilation of her cervix and frequent contractions that began occurring early into her pregnancy.

As a result, she was required to undergo a medical procedure called a "cervical cerclage" to prevent premature birth of our daughter. The procedure was successful and our daughter who is now pursuing a master's degree in a medical pathology field was born full-term.

I was able to secure regional distribution for the fishing accessory in Wal-Mart stores and I landed a promotion for the product with a major oil company who used the product to increase sales of their outboard motor oil by placing a unit in each case they manufactured. These sales gave us corporate capitol to increase our marketing and I began being paid a small monthly salary by the corporation. My partners knew that my time was valuable and that I needed ample time during normal business hours, to promote the product and to increase sales by continued representation of the product to new outlets and to remain in contact with those already carrying it. Not long afterward, I also secured distribution for the product through Bass Pro Shops, Cabela's and Academy Stores. We eventually licensed the product to a large fishing tackle conglomerate.

13

TTI Blakemore Corporation took the product on and still pays us monthly royalties from sales that accrue through these same outlets.

A Perfect Fit

I resigned my position with the specialty food company and looked for work I could perform on-the-side, during hours that would not affect the marketing of the fishing tackle accessory. I found an ad by a publishing company, seeking a contract newspaper distributor and I was hired to perform the early morning deliveries and the associated paperwork during available hours when I was not involved in the product marketing. It was a perfect fit and over time, I actually began to enjoy the newspaper distribution position.

CHAPTER TWO

Collection Time Shenanigans

After being interviewed for the contract newspaper carrier position, at my home, by the District Manager (DM), I was hired for the position. I remember upon first showing up at the site where newspapers were dropped each morning, to be disbursed by carriers, that several of them approached me, warning that the DM was extremely dishonest and that he would take every possible opportunity to cheat you out of money. They also added that the main office knew about his corrupt practices but that they had no intention of firing him or reprimanding him for them because he was achieving circulation increases for the company. I did not believe the accusations and I came to the conclusion at the time, that these were simply carriers who were disgruntled with the company for whatever reasons.

At the end of my first month of contract services as a newspaper carrier for the company, the DM came to collect from me.

He would have me pay the difference between what I had collected from my customers, versus what I owed the company once my unsold newspapers were credited off of the balance due. He calculated these figures and computed the amount I owed the company for the current month due and asked me to pay him cash. This struck me a bit strange and so I asked him why he was asking for a cash-payment. He replied by saying that it simply made it easier for him to pay the main office a lump sum he would collect from all carriers combined, rather than having to take a number of different personal checks back to the main office with him. This sounded logical and my wife and I agreed to pay the cash to settle our first month's bill. Afterward however, we decided that it was better for us to have a canceled check for tax-record purposes and that when he came back on the next month's collection date, we would simply tell him this.

An Emerging Pattern of Dishonesty

When the next end-of-month rolled around, we explained this to the DM and he agreed but he then asked if we would make checks payable to his name, rather than to the company's name.

With a second strange request being made I began to feel uncomfortable but I agreed to the request, since he was willing to accept a check, rather than cash. Being a new contract carrier, I didn't understand the newspaper business well enough to recognize that this was not a proper way for the DM to collect from me. What really placed me on alert however, was the fact that within days of my making the payment to him, he arrived at my home claiming he had made a mistake during the collections and that he needed an additional sum of money (relatively small) to turn in to the main office, to completely settle my balance-due. He also added that he had made up for the difference out of his own pocket and needed the payment for reimbursement.

I again agreed to make the payment but by this time I had developed a strong mistrust for this DM. While looking at a past statement, I found written in small print at the bottom of it, directions stating to the effect that contract carriers were to make checks payable, only to the company. This gave me further substantiation for the feelings of mistrust I had developed for this man.

Looking Out for my Interests

I began to understand my statement better in-general, involving newspapers provided me and credits applied to my bill, leaving the difference I would owe each month. I began to go over these with a fine toothed comb so-to-speak, to make sure that the amount the DM collected from me was also the amount he was actually turning in to the main office. About one year later, the manager over the circulation department and this DM's boss called me, asking if I would take a DM position that was open in another area but with my other responsibilities at the time, I politely refused the job (it would be offered to me again later).

While I was on the phone with him however, I mentioned that the DM who was collecting from me, was having me make my checks payable to him. The circulation manager immediately pointed out that this is not what he was supposed to be doing and that I could refuse to do so if I wished. I was floored when he added that this same DM was caught skimming money from collections that were due to the company.

This required him to pay the company back on two previous occasions for money he had basically embezzled.

Increasing Circulation Covers a Multitude of Sins

This corrupt DM was also known for turning-in many new customer orders, increasing subscriber circulation and winning yearly contests among his peers for doing-so and this apparently was the reason the company allowed the questionable practices to continue for years following. The company did however require the DM to repay monies he had obtained from them illegally but they did not appear to be concerned about monies he had cheated carriers out of during that same period of time. This brings me to another unethical practice this DM was involved in that I will cover in the next chapter and one that the company would not resolve, in spite of numerous complaints from many carriers over several years period of time.

CHAPTER THREE

Tucked Away for a Rainy Day

Performing the duties of a newspaper carrier requires use of delivery supplies, including rubber bands and plastic bags to protect newspapers delivered during wet weather conditions. This is true of both home subscriber customers and stores that are delivered early mornings before they have opened for business. These supplies were sold to carriers by the newspaper company as they needed them with the cost of the supplies being applied to their monthly statements.

Fellow contract carriers began to approach me frequently, claiming that supplies they had not ordered nor received were showing up as charges on their monthly statements, sometimes amounting to 100s of dollars. Eventually, the same thing happened to me as well and I questioned the DM about it. He responded by saying that the supplies were some I had ordered months previously and that the main office had somehow failed to make the appropriate charges at the time.

Oh what a Tangled Web we Weave

I accepted this explanation being given by the
DM at the time however, within a month or two
of these charges being explained to me, I ordered
new supplies. Upon these being delivered to me
by the DM, he asked that I pay for them by cash
or check, rather than charges for them being
applied to my upcoming statement. He added that
this is how the company wanted him to handle
supplies being sold to contract carriers for the
time being. I decided this time, that I would call
someone in management at the circulation
department to confirm that I was actually
supposed to pay for the supplies upfront. I was
told that they were unaware of any such directive
being given to DMs regarding supplies to contract
carriers, which confirmed my suspicion that this
was not supposed to be occurring.

An Insult to the Intelligence

It was not difficult to figure out the type of scam
that was being perpetrated and in some ways;
these types of issues were insulting to one's
intelligence. Apparently, there is the belief by
some in the newspaper business, that contract
carriers are people who lack intelligence.

It is believed that they are all people who come from a very low-class background. While this certainly can be the case (regardless of occupation), I personally worked with fellow contract carriers who were well-known retired businessmen or who were police officers or managers of other businesses and delivered newspapers as supplemental jobs.

In regard to the bogus supplies charges, the DM was simply signing for supplies at the main office and applying charges for them, to carriers who had not actually ordered them. He would then take the supplies that would be paid-for via these charges and would re-sell them to other carriers for cash payments. While I did not confront the DM with this revelation specifically, I did tell him that I would no longer pay for supplies upfront but that I would require that they be applied as charges to my monthly statements. I also added that I intended to keep up with my supply orders very closely.

Amazingly, this was all it took to stop the bogus charges from intermittently showing up on my monthly statements. A new type of bogus charge eventually began showing up on carrier's monthly statements.

This scam however, not only added potential bonus compensation to the DM but also increased newspaper circulation numbers illegitimately. In addition to this, a newly-devised plan involving discontinued home subscriber customers also began to occur. I will give detail to these other scams that were being perpetrated, to benefit both the income and circulation of the publishing company, in chapters that follow.

Outfoxing the Fox

It began to appear as if new scams were continually being devised as old ones were being figured-out by the contract carriers. Our main defenses against these practices were to either resign our contracts (which many did) or to watch our monthly statements very closely and to go over them in detail to catch any bogus activity that might be occurring on them. I chose the latter approach because the work fit-well into my other activities and I did not want to be a quitter. The job was also one of self-employment and logically required diligence in self-representation of the contract-carrier side of the business agreement. Being self-employed requires a degree of self-advocacy in order to survive these types of issues.

CHAPTER FOUR

**How to Increase Newspaper Circulation
without even Trying**

With my being the carrier with the largest
delivery territory, the publishing company
required a few extra duties of me. They placed a
toll-free number telephone in my home, so that I
could take complaints from customers who
missed their deliveries or who were seeking
subscriber information. I also handed-out any
complaints to fellow carriers that came in on the
phone line, each previous morning. At one point,
carriers began to complain frequently that
newspapers were not being discontinued from
their daily count, even after they had turned-in
delivery stops on them. These were those who
failed to pay their delivery bill or who had moved
or passed away, etc…

Delivering Newspapers to the Dead

Some of the carriers were showing me that these
discontinued subscribers, no longer being
delivered were mounting up into the dozens, even
with repeated stops being placed on them, via the
proper paperwork.

Phone calls to the main office were also not getting these stopped. I eventually asked the DM why this was occurring and he stated that the main office was not allowing stops at that time because they wanted to achieve an increase over the previous year's circulation. The only problem with this plan was the fact that the carriers were still being charged for these customers, which in some cases added 100s of dollars to their statements each month. Some carriers actually resigned over the issue as others did due to other past issues involving dishonesty in the company.

The DM devised a solution to this problem but one I was very uncomfortable with. Since my routes included those that I delivered to single copy customers (stores and news racks) and since I was reimbursed for any unsold newspapers, I could simply turn-in these carrier's undelivered newspapers on my paperwork for credit, so that they would no longer be paying for them. At the same time, home subscriber circulation would not decrease. This was the instruction I received from the DM and that he had me to continue doing over the next three years.

I asked him when this first began, if he would take responsibility for instructing the carriers to turn these in to me and he assured me that he would. I also called the man who was zone manager at the time and asked him if I should be following this instruction by the DM and he told me to continue following the instructions.

Documentation... Documentation... Documentation!

Despite this fact, in order to safeguard against blame being shifted to me should the practice be investigated at any point, I asked each carrier to sign a sheet stating to the effect that they were turning these undelivered newspapers over to me for credit at the DM's instruction. I also saved all canceled checks I paid to each carrier, which amounted to 1,000s of dollars over a three year period.

I eventually complained enough about the length of time that this practice was being continued that the DM finally agreed to place stops on discontinued customers for these carriers rather than continuing the home subscriber circulation scam.

Not long following discontinuation of paying for carrier's undelivered newspapers, a new scam emerged, this time directly affecting income-credit due to single copy carriers. We were in-essence being cheated out of income due to us for our delivery services to stores and news racks (single copy sales). The DM and whoever else was involved in this scam began "charging back" carriers for unsold newspapers, turned-in by them at the end of each month for credit. Carriers would turn in their unsold newspapers, logging them onto a sheet that calculated the amount of credit due to them that would be subtracted from their monthly statements. Carriers with single copy sales on their routes began to complain to me, that they were being charged-back for unsold newspapers they were turning in and I responded by letting them know that the same thing was happening to me as well.

When Honesty is not Welcome

It was during this time that a new DM was assigned over the area that included my routes and those of these other carriers. This man was refreshingly honest in his practices and he showed genuine concern for what was occurring regarding the charge-backs.

When I mentioned the complaints I was hearing from other carriers, he stated that carriers throughout his district were being charged-back for returns, for several months running, with the implied reason being that the main office was finding discrepancies in the numbers of unsold newspapers being turned in.

We both agreed that this many carriers could not possibly all be giving incorrect calculations for several consecutive months and that this appeared to be a bogus method for increasing single copy circulation. Some of these carriers were adamant that they were not miscounting returns in their own favor and that in some cases they recounted them several times or had a family member recount them for accuracy before turning them in.

The new DM and his Zone Manager (also an honest man), decided that they would run an experiment on the issue, using my returns and those of other carrier's on the test. When they came to collect my next month's returns, they would personally count them, before turning them over to the main office, to see if they would still show a discrepancy and a charge-back.

Amazingly, the charge-backs did appear again and this was confirmation to these managers that there was indeed a scam involving bogus charge-backs occurring. Not long following this incident, the Zone Manager resigned his job and the DM was fired from his.

These two men were not the only honest employees who worked for the publishing company but who resigned or were fired due to issues of dishonesty they were witnessing. There was another DM, who was promoted to a Zone Management position as well, who also eventually resigned with the newspaper after many months of attempting to convince the heads of the company to correct the methods of dishonesty that were occurring.

As I write this chapter, I recall receiving an email from this man, just last week, in which he reminded me that he could no longer continue with a company whose standard was that of deceit. I admire him for taking the stance that he did, as these other men did. I believe much of what drove this man's convictions of honesty are centered in the fact that he is a Christian man (now a full time Minister) and retired from honorable service with the U.S. military.

An Offer I couldn't Refuse

There was a point in time in which I-too resigned within two weeks of being hired for a DM position and afterward I returned to a contract delivery position. The turnover of both contract carrier and management positions was incredibly frequent and logically, this was due to the issues that were occurring within the company. I literally saw a dozen DMs come and go in less than two years at one point and my own reason for resigning was due to yet another issue of dishonesty as well.

I was offered a district management territory that included several cities with relatively large populations within it. A number of DMs who had resigned the district complained that it was too large and impossible for one person to handle. I was notified of the position and offered the district with one of the larger cities being taken off of it.

The circulation manager, who hired me, even stated that with the district being reduced in size, it would be far less of a headache for a new DM.

I accepted the position under the revised circumstances and once I was fully trained, I was informed that the city was added back into the district. I basically felt as if I was tricked into accepting the position and I resigned it as a result. Amazingly, they called me a short time later, asking if I would take a contract delivery territory for which I agreed. It was obvious that the company often operated in a mode of desperation due to the frequency of managers and carriers resigning.

CHAPTER FIVE

Confessions of a Corrupt District Manager

As mentioned previously, the first DM I witnessed perpetrating dishonest business practices was eventually fired from his job. The company had apparently allowed his corrupt behaviors to the fullest extent possible but once enough fingers began to be pointed at the company itself, it was time for a little housecleaning. There was also likely the fear that a DM would have the ability to implement other company representatives as holding some responsibility for their dishonest practices.

Prior to his being fired, the DM began to run routes that were resigned by carriers, while keeping the monthly pay customer payments as personal profit. Company policy did not allow DMs to keep monies received from down routes but it was to be turned-in to a company fund. The DM found a way around this policy by making it appear that a carrier was contracted on a down route, while he himself was actually delivering it. At times, I was the carrier he showed to be on a down route.

This was done while he received the profits from it and I eventually discovered this rather inadvertently.

The DM would approach me early mornings while I was picking up my newspapers at the drop-site and he would ask me to sign a blank contract. He claimed that my original contract was misplaced at the main office and that this would place it back on file. I was highly suspicious of this request due to his past behaviors but I agreed to sign the contract. A few days later he appeared at my home to inform me that he sent out bills to monthly pay customers on a down route and that he used my name and address for them to remit payment to. He asked that I cash the checks as they came in and turn the payments over to him.

How about a little Tax Evasion?

I immediately figured out what he was doing and I asked him if he realized that I would have to report the income as my own and pay taxes on it at the end of the year. His answer in-response to this question was that I shouldn't report it and with the income actually not belonging to me, I didn't report it.

While the payments totaled just under $1,000.00 this still amounted to yet one more feather in his hat of corruption, being that of tax evasion, in addition to breaking company policy, among other things. There were times I would be in phone conversation with the circulation manager and he would thank me for filling-in on down routes to help the DM between finding new carriers. These were down routes I knew for a fact I had not filled in on.

A few weeks prior to the DM being asked to leave the company, I was standing alone with him in my front yard and I basically asked him why he committed so much dishonesty in his business practices. He literally displayed a look of regret on his face as he opened-up to me and began to admit that he was involved in a great deal of corruption and that the company was allowing it, as long as he kept the circulation numbers increased in his district. He further answered my question by saying that he struggled with an anguishing fear that he would not make enough money and as a result that he might lose his wife. He added that he found a number of ways to insure that he made sufficient income.

I was shocked by the fact that he was confessing this to me but at the same time I had no sympathy for him whatsoever and found no legitimacy in his excuse.

Amazingly, a circulation manager who had somewhat befriended me, after my many years as a contract carrier for the company, made a similar admission to me by phone on one occasion. Knowing I was a Christian, he stated to me that he regretted many of the things he had resorted to in his business practices with the company. I only hope these same confessions were offered to the ears of God and that true repentance followed them, especially with the fact that he-too was a professing Christian. Shortly before my wife and I resigned our contracts with the company, she happened to be speaking to this same circulation manager on the phone regarding issues we were experiencing. He made a statement to us that again came as somewhat of a shock. In reference to the fact that the company was beginning to struggle to meet budgets and were feverishly finding every possible avenue to increase revenues, including downsizing their work force, he simply stated to her that we should "watch our backs" (verbatim quote).

This was his way of indirectly warning us that we could be on the receiving end of further corrupt activities. Within months of that phone call, we resigned due to credit balances due to us being withheld and delayed, which permanently ended our association with the company.

CHAPTER SIX

Ghost Routes Galore

As economic changes and internet availability of news began to negatively affect printed newspaper companies, many of them began to downsize their delivery areas and their base of employees. The newspaper I served as contract carrier for was no exception and one of the first things to go with their downsizing efforts were "rural customers" (those outside of city limits). There were a number of rural routes discontinued, just outside of the areas where I was delivering to customers in the suburbs.

The company apparently had a brainstorm and decided to devise a plan that would allow them to continue showing these customers from the discontinued routes, as being current ones, to prevent a reduction in home subscriber circulation numbers. They simply added the names and addresses of these customers from the discontinued routes, to my monthly statements. The newspapers themselves were stopped and were not being sent out to be delivered but the paperwork showed that they were.

Each of these rural customers would be listed on my monthly statements, including charges to me for the newspapers I was not getting, for over a year and a half following discontinued delivery to them. The new DM at the time, informed me that the company had made these same type revisions by adding discontinued rural customers to other carrier's lists in his district.

A Purposeful Glitch in the System

When this manipulation of the rural customer lists first began to occur and upon my complaining about it to the main office, I was told that it was a temporary development that was occurring due to changes in their accounting system but that it would soon be resolved. This again was seemingly an insult to my intelligence because customers from a different route, that are all under different route-numbers and contract carrier's names, do not transfer to other routes unless done-so intentionally. It was also obvious that the scam was being perpetrated in order to prevent a sudden and significant reduction in circulation numbers.

This was especially obvious with the fact that this continued for over 18 months.

A new DM was placed over the district and he began attempting to get the issue resolved because it was negatively affecting my credit balance by 100s of dollars per month and these charges for rural customer newspapers were not being credited back to me. When the past credit due to me and my wife who had also been delivering routes by that time for approximately five years and who also had rural customers added to her statements reached over $4,000.00, we let the new DM know that we would be resigning as a result of it. He then decided to send a memo directly to the circulation manager, detailing these bogus charges and requesting that we be issued checks to cover them, immediately, in exchange for us remaining under contract.

Resolved by a Memo

This was not the first time the circulation manager was informed of the issue, in-fact I had personally spoken to him about it as well but the memo was the step that succeeded (I still retain a copy of it) and we were finally compensated for the bogus rural customer charges.

While the company corrected the issue with us, this still does not take away from the fact that a dishonest circulation scam was taking place and that the publishing company was not held accountable for their unethical business practices.

As mentioned in my introduction, I firmly believe that accountability for dishonest actions is sometimes delayed but never escaped. While I personally hold no grudge against any of these individuals I am also confident in divine judgment. My personal hope is that these individuals have repented of their deeds and are moving forward in honest pursuits and this I state with absolute sincerely.

The Last Straw

Some months following correction of the previously described issue involving scam circulation increases, other issues began to develop, affecting both my mine and my wife's credit balances as contract carriers. Once again, this was tantamount to taking food out of our family's mouths. I had warned the company that if such issues began to occur again, that we would resign our contracts without notice and this is what eventually occurred.

Normally, early resignation without proper notice will bring a penalty/fine to a contract carrier, according to the company's policies.

Upon our resignation, I firmly suggested that the company accept a "clean break" from us; in addition to paying us for all past-due credit balances we were owed. They abided by the request which we forwarded to them through a mediating bureau and they resolved the issue on an immediate basis. Their promptness was almost certainly due to the fact that I warned of further reporting to additional agencies should they have not accepted our terms of resignation.

CONCLUSION:

I am not so naive as to not recognize that corruption in business has always existed and will continue to exist throughout this dispensation of mankind. I do however believe that the legal avenues in-place that provides opportunity to remedy some of these issues is often not resorted-to. I must point a finger of guilt at myself in this regard because I failed to act sooner and as often as I should have. In many cases it is simply a matter of victims not wanting to experience the stress of reporting illegal practices.

For others it may be a matter of not really caring about issues of dishonestly being perpetrated in business if it does not directly affect them. Fear of reprisals as previously mentioned is yet another reason businesses may not be called into accountability by observers of their unethical behaviors.

The Leaven of Corruption

Regardless of the reasons corruption may be allowed to continue within companies, this often gives it opportunity to grow and continue to increase in incidence, which can eventually affect societies as a whole.

A very wise man once said *"A little leaven leavens the whole lump of dough."* – meaning the yeast of corruption, when left to work, can eventually take over the whole ball of dough.

It is my hope that the preceding chapters of this book help to inspire others to step forward in self-advocacy against dishonest business practices and to also do-so on the behalf of others who might eventually be affected by it. When honest people join together to bring about accountability for corrupt business practices, changes can take place and differences can be made.

(END)